AI-Powered Business

A Comprehensive Guide to Transforming Your Enterprise

M.A. Gorre

Contents

Preface   V

1. Introduction   1

2. Artificial Intelligence and Machine Learning   4

3. Understanding Data: Types, Sources, and Structures   8

4. Data Ethics, Privacy, and Security   13

5. Business Readiness and Strategy   18

6. AI Readiness Checklists   23

7. Resource Inventory   29

8. Creating an AI-Driven Business Strategy   34

9. Measuring ROI and Key Performance Indicators   40

10. Talent and Team Structure   45

11. Training and Development for AI Skills   52

12. Data Infrastructure and Engineering   57

13. Data Storage and Database Management   62

14. Data Cleaning, Transformation, and Preprocessing   67

15. Algorithms, Models, and Applications   72

16. Sector-Specific Case Studies   88

17. Operationalization and Scaling   93

18. Future Trends and Long-Term Strategy   104

19. Resources   109

20. Appendix   113

21. Sample Data Science Project Timelines and Budgets   115

Preface

Why This Book Exists

In today's rapidly evolving landscape, where data reigns and informs almost every decision, understanding how to leverage Artificial Intelligence (AI) for business success is no longer optional—it's imperative. As we move deeper into the era of big data, machine learning, and predictive analytics, the divide between companies that "get it" and those that don't is widening. This book is designed to serve as a comprehensive guide for business leaders, decision-makers, and professionals who aim to bridge that gap and turn data into actionable insights.

Who Should Read This Book?

- **C-Suite Executives**: Understand how AI can offer strategic advantages, improve ROI, and foster innovation.

- **Managers and Team Leads**: Learn how to assemble and manage an AI-focused team, and how to integrate AI into your existing workflows.

- **Data Scientists and Engineers**: Acquaint yourselves with the business aspects and challenges in implementing AI solutions.

- **Consultants and Strategists**: Find case studies and frameworks to advise your clients more effectively on AI adoption.

What You Will Learn

- **The Basics**: A solid grounding in what AI and data management entail.

- **Business Strategy**: How to align your business strategy with AI capabilities.

- **Technical Insights**: A look into the algorithms and data structures that make AI possible.

- **Implementation**: Step-by-step guides on how to implement AI into your business operations.

- **Future Trends**: What to watch out for and how to stay ahead of the curve.

How to Use This Book

This book is organized into several parts, each catering to different aspects of business and AI. Whether you're a novice just dipping your toes in the AI waters, or an expert looking for more advanced strategies and insights, you can either read the book cover to cover or focus on the chapters most relevant to your needs.

- **Beginners**: Parts I and II offer a fundamental understanding of AI and how to prepare your business for AI integration.

- **Intermediate Readers**: Parts III through V delve into the nitty-gritty of data management, algorithms, and business-specific applications.

- **Advanced Readers**: Parts VI and VII focus on case studies, operationalization, and future trends.

Chapter One

Introduction

N avigating the AI-Driven Business Landscape

The New Frontier

Welcome to the world of Artificial Intelligence, a landscape that is reshaping businesses across the globe. If the first wave of the digital revolution was led by the internet and mobile technology, the next wave is undoubtedly powered by AI. From automated customer service and supply chain optimization to predictive analytics and personalized marketing, AI is rapidly becoming an indispensable tool for business success. But as we navigate through this transformative era, the fundamental question for business leaders remains: How can AI be leveraged effectively to gain a competitive edge?

Why AI, Why Now?

While AI technology has been around for several decades, recent advancements in computational power, data storage, and algorithmic design have catapulted AI from academic research labs into corporate boardrooms. No longer is it a futuristic notion; AI is here and now, and its applications are vast and ever-expanding.

The Data Imperative

In an AI-driven world, data is the new oil. It fuels the algorithms and models that make AI so powerful. But, much like crude oil, raw data is of limited value unless refined and utilized effectively. This book aims to guide you through the process of collecting, managing, and leveraging data to inform and drive business decisions.

What This Book Offers

1. **Comprehensive Coverage**: From the basics of AI and data to advanced strategies for implementation and scaling, this book aims to be a one-stop-shop for all things AI in business.

2. **Practical Insights**: Go beyond theoretical concepts with real-world case studies and step-by-step guides to implementing AI solutions.

3. **Business-centric**: Tailored specifically for business leaders and decision-makers, the book addresses the unique challenges and opportunities that AI presents in a business context.

How to Approach This Book

"Data-Driven: Harnessing AI for Business Success" is designed to be modular. Each section builds upon the last, but they are also intended to stand alone, making it easy to focus on the areas most relevant to you and your business. Whether you are new to AI or looking to deepen your understanding, this book offers a pathway for everyone.

- **For the Uninitiated**: If you're new to the world of AI, start with Part I for an overview and basic understanding.

- **For the Experienced**: If you're already familiar with AI fundamentals but are looking to understand how to apply these to your business, jump ahead to Part III or IV.

- **For the Visionary**: If you're interested in understanding the future landscape of AI in business, don't miss Part VIII.

Navigating the Future

The aim of this book is not just to educate but to prepare you for the future—a future that is already unfolding. By harnessing the power of AI, you're not just adopting new technology; you're embracing a paradigm shift that will define the business landscape for decades to come.

Chapter Two

Artificial Intelligence and Machine Learning

Definitions and Key Distinctions

Artificial Intelligence

Artificial Intelligence (AI) refers to the simulation of human intelligence in machines programmed to think, reason, learn, and solve problems. Essentially, AI aims to create a machine that can perform tasks that would ordinarily require human intelligence—such as understanding natural language, recognizing patterns, solving problems, and making decisions.

Machine Learning

Machine Learning (ML), a subset of AI, provides the foundation for the machine's ability to learn from data, improving its performance over time without being explicitly programmed. In ML, algorithms are used to find patterns or regularities in data. In simpler terms, machine learning enables computers to carry out tasks by learning from data, instead of following pre-defined rules.

Key Distinctions

1. **Scope**: AI has a broader scope encompassing anything that allows computers to mimic human intelligence, including robotics, problem-solving, and speech recognition. ML is specifically focused on the development of algorithms to enable learning from data.

2. **Learning**: AI doesn't always have to learn from data. For instance, rule-based expert systems make decisions based on a set of explicit rules. ML specifically learns from data; as more data becomes available, an ML system can learn from it and improve.

3. **Goal**: The primary aim of AI is to create intelligent systems that can perform tasks without human intervention. ML aims to enable machines to learn from data so that they can give accurate predictions or decisions.

A Brief History

The Dawn of AI

The concept of artificial intelligence has been around for a very long time—think ancient myths of automatons endowed with human-like intelligence. However, AI as a field of scientific inquiry was born in the mid-20th century. The term 'Artificial Intelligence' was coined by John McCarthy for the famous 1956 Dartmouth Workshop, which is considered the founding event of AI as an academic subject.

Key Milestones in AI and ML

1. **1950s - Early Foundations**: Alan Turing laid the theoretical foundation for both artificial intelligence and machine learning with his Turing Test in the early '50s.

2. **1960s - Rule-Based Systems**: The first AI programs, which used rule-based systems to make 'intelligent' decisions, were created.

3. **1970s - AI Winter**: Overshadowed by the inability to fulfill exaggerated expectations, AI research funding was cut, leading to what is known as the first AI winter.

4. **1980s - Revival and Expert Systems**: A revival came in the form of expert systems, rule-based systems that mimicked the decision-making abilities of a human expert.

5. **1990s - Machine Learning Takes Off**: Algorithms like backpropagation for neural networks were invented, allowing machines to learn from data, marking the ascendance of machine learning as a field.

6. **2000s - Big Data and Improved Algorithms**: With the explosion of data and increasing computational power, more complex algorithms that could process massive amounts of data were developed.

7. **2010s - Deep Learning Revolution**: Deep learning, a subset of machine learning with architectures inspired by the human brain, gained prominence. This led to significant improvements in tasks like image and speech recognition.

8. **2020s - Towards AGI?**: The focus is now shifting toward developing General AI, machines that can perform any intellectual task that a human can do.

The Modern Landscape

Today, AI and ML technologies power everything from search engine algorithms and recommendation systems to autonomous vehicles and personalized medicine. The progress in these fields continues to accelerate, driven by advances in computing power and the availability of increasingly large datasets.

Chapter Three

Understanding Data: Types, Sources, and Structures

D ata is often likened to oil—a raw resource that holds immense potential value but requires refining to unleash its true power. Understanding the different types of data, where it comes from, and how it is structured is essential for anyone looking to leverage Artificial Intelligence (AI) and Machine Learning (ML) for business success.

Structured vs. Unstructured Data

Structured Data

Structured data is organized and formatted in a way that it's easily searchable in relational databases. Examples include spreadsheets where data is arranged in rows and columns, or databases where data is stored in fields. Typical formats include numbers, dates, and strings.

Advantages:

- Easy to query and analyze.

- Suitable for machine learning models that require labeled data.

Disadvantages:

- Limited in complexity.

- May not capture the richness or depth of human experience.

Unstructured Data

Unstructured data is the opposite: it's not organized in a pre-defined manner or doesn't have a pre-defined data model. This category encompasses texts, images, sound, video, etc.

Advantages:

- Rich and deep, capturing a broad spectrum of information.

- Allows for complex analyses and pattern discovery.

Disadvantages:

- Difficult to sort and analyze.

- Requires more advanced tools and methods for processing.

Semi-Structured Data

A middle ground between structured and unstructured data, semi-structured data has elements of both. For instance, an XML or JSON file can have both structured and unstructured elements.

Data Taxonomy

Numerical Data

This data type can be divided into two categories:

1. **Discrete Data**: Specific, countable values. E.g., the number of employees in a company.

2. **Continuous Data**: Any value within a range. E.g., temperature readings.

Categorical Data

Data that can be sorted into categories or groups:

1. **Ordinal Data**: Categories have a meaningful order but the distance between the categories is not known. E.g., ratings of 'poor', 'average', 'good'.

2. **Nominal Data**: Categories don't have a meaningful order. E.g., gender, types of fruits.

Textual Data

String formats, usually consisting of words or alphanumeric characters. E.g., customer reviews, tweets.

Multimedia Data

Incorporates audio, visual, and other sensory data:

1. **Image Data**: E.g., customer photos, product images.

2. **Audio Data**: E.g., customer service calls, podcasts.

3. **Video Data**: E.g., CCTV footage, user-generated content.

Time-Series Data

Data points collected or recorded at a time interval. E.g., stock prices, weather data.

Spatial Data

Information representing physical locations. E.g., GPS coordinates, maps.

Sources of Data

1. **Internal Sources**: Data generated within the organization. E.g., sales records, employee performance metrics.

2. **External Sources**: Publicly available or purchased data. E. g., market trends, social media chatter.

3. **Generated Data**: Created through operations and interac-

tions, often in real-time. E.g., sensor readings, user activity logs.

Understanding the nature of data, its taxonomy, and sources provides a foundational knowledge base that is essential for anyone interested in utilizing AI and ML effectively. This foundation enables business leaders and technical experts alike to identify what kind of data they need, how to collect it, and ultimately, how to use it for informed decision-making.

Chapter Four

Data Ethics, Privacy, and Security

I n an age where data is often compared to oil, the ethical dimensions of collecting, storing, and using data can't be overstated. Equally crucial are privacy and security concerns. Below, we'll explore these facets in depth to provide a comprehensive understanding of data ethics, privacy, and security in the context of business applications of AI and machine learning.

Ethical Considerations

Informed Consent

Whenever data is collected, especially from individuals, they should be fully informed about how their data will be used, stored, and shared.

This establishes a foundational layer of trust and also protects businesses from legal repercussions.

Data Minimization

Collect only the data that is absolutely necessary for the objectives at hand. Excessive data collection not only exposes businesses to unnecessary risks but also may breach ethical norms.

Fairness and Bias

AI and machine learning models can inadvertently perpetuate existing biases present in the data or in the human designers of the algorithms. Businesses need to take steps to identify and eliminate bias in their data-driven systems.

Transparency and Accountability

When AI systems make decisions, especially those that affect human lives or livelihoods, it's crucial for businesses to be transparent about how decisions are made and be accountable for errors or malfeasance.

Data Stewardship

Organizations have an ethical responsibility to protect the data they collect and to ensure it's used responsibly. This includes anonymizing data to protect individual identities and ensuring data is not misused for malicious intents.

Privacy

Data Encryption

The encryption of data is a primary method for ensuring privacy. This is especially relevant for sensitive data like financial records or personal information.

Anonymization

Data should be anonymized whenever possible, removing all personally identifiable information where it's not essential to the task.

Data Rights

Individuals from whom data is collected should have a clear understanding of their rights concerning that data, including the right to have their data deleted.

Security

Data Access Controls

Not everyone in an organization should have access to all data. Access should be based on roles and necessity, and logs should be kept to monitor who accessed what data and when.

Regular Audits

Regular security audits can identify vulnerabilities before they can be exploited, offering opportunities for preventative action.

Incident Response Plans

In the event of a data breach or other security incident, a well-documented and rehearsed incident response plan can minimize damage and restore normal operations more quickly.

Regulatory Frameworks

GDPR (General Data Protection Regulation)

For businesses operating in or dealing with citizens of the European Union, GDPR imposes strict rules about data collection and use, including giving individuals the "right to be forgotten."

CCPA (California Consumer Privacy Act)

Similar to GDPR but specific to California, CCPA gives consumers more control over their personal data.

HIPAA (Health Insurance Portability and Accountability Act)

For healthcare-related data in the United States, HIPAA provides a framework for safeguarding medical information.

Sector-Specific Regulations

Depending on the industry, there may be additional frameworks or guidelines to consider, such as PCI-DSS for payment card information or FERPA for educational records.

Understanding and adhering to ethical standards, privacy protocols, and security measures not only protect businesses from legal trouble but also endear them to customers by demonstrating responsibility and integrity. This is increasingly vital in our data-driven world, where lapses in any of these areas can have significant reputational and financial consequences.

Chapter Five

Business Readiness and Strategy

E valuating Business Readiness for AI

    The decision to implement AI and machine learning into your business model is both exciting and daunting. While the potential for transformation is immense, the pathway is fraught with challenges and intricacies. For this reason, a careful evaluation of business readiness is paramount. Below is a comprehensive look at how to evaluate your business's preparedness for adopting AI.

Understanding AI's Value Proposition

Assessing Business Needs

Before diving into AI, the foremost step is identifying the areas where AI can bring actual value. Are you looking to streamline operations, enhance customer experiences, or perhaps break into new markets? Having a clear idea of your business needs will serve as the cornerstone of your AI strategy.

Cost-Benefit Analysis

The next logical step is a thorough cost-benefit analysis. You'll need to factor in not just the direct costs like software licenses and hardware but also indirect ones such as employee training and potential downtime.

Infrastructure Readiness

Computing Power

Machine learning models, especially deep learning ones, require significant computational power. Does your existing infrastructure support this, or would you need to invest in additional resources?

Data Storage

Machine learning is data-hungry. Do you have the necessary storage solutions to handle large volumes of data securely and efficiently?

Data Preparedness

Data Quality

Garbage in, garbage out—this adage holds especially true for AI. Do you have access to high-quality, relevant data that can be used for training machine learning models?

Data Governance

Who owns the data? How is it managed, and who has access to it? The importance of a well-defined data governance policy can't be overstated.

Skills and Talent

In-House vs. Outsourcing

Do you have the necessary skill sets within your organization to develop, deploy, and maintain AI solutions, or will you need to outsource?

Training and Development

Adopting AI may require upskilling your existing workforce. What plans do you have for training and development?

Regulatory and Ethical Compliance

We've previously discussed the importance of data ethics, privacy, and security. Understanding and adhering to regional and industry-specific regulations is critical.

Change Management

Employee Resistance

Change is often met with resistance. How prepared are you to manage the cultural shift that comes with AI adoption?

Success Metrics

How will you measure the success or failure of your AI initiatives? Having clear KPIs (Key Performance Indicators) in place is crucial for gauging progress.

Pilot Testing

Before full-scale implementation, conducting pilot tests on smaller scales can help in identifying potential hitches and provide real-world insights into how the system performs.

Long-Term Strategy

Scalability

Is your AI solution scalable? As your business grows, your AI system should be capable of growing with it.

Sustainability

AI is not a one-off project but a long-term strategy. Do you have plans for maintaining and updating your AI systems?

Innovation Roadmap

AI is a rapidly evolving field. Does your business strategy account for future advancements and innovations?

By thoroughly evaluating each of the above facets, you can gauge your organization's readiness to adopt AI effectively. This evaluation serves as the blueprint for your AI journey, helping to mitigate risks, optimize costs, and most importantly, align your AI initiatives with your broader business objectives.

Chapter Six

AI Readiness Checklists

A Comprehensive Guide

Adopting Artificial Intelligence (AI) into your business is not a minor endeavor. To ensure that you are well-prepared for this transformative journey, a comprehensive checklist can serve as your roadmap. Below is a detailed checklist covering all facets of business readiness for AI adoption.

Understanding the Business Needs

- Clearly define the problem(s) you aim to solve with AI.

- Identify key business processes that can benefit from AI.

- Perform a SWOT analysis focusing on AI adoption.

- Conduct a cost-benefit analysis.

- Align AI goals with overall business objectives.

Infrastructure and Technical Readiness

Computing Resources

- Assess current computing capabilities.

- Estimate additional computational needs.

- Budget for and acquire necessary hardware or cloud resources.

Data Storage

- Evaluate current data storage solutions.

- Estimate storage needs for AI data.

- Explore options for scalable data storage solutions.

Network Infrastructure

- Assess network bandwidth and latency.

- Consider the requirements for data transfer and real-time processing.

- Strengthen network security protocols.

Data Preparedness

Data Audit

- Identify existing data sources relevant to the AI project.

- Perform a data quality audit.

- Catalog and index data resources.

Data Governance

- Establish data ownership protocols.

- Create data access and management policies.

- Define data retention and deletion policies.

Talent and Skill Sets

- Identify internal team members interested in AI.

- Evaluate the need for hiring external AI specialists.

- Plan for training and skill development for existing employees.

- Decide on the need for consultants or outsourced teams.

Regulatory and Ethical Compliance

- Familiarize yourself with applicable data protection laws (GDPR, CCPA, etc.).

- Conduct an ethical review focusing on data collection, use, and bias.

- Prepare compliance documentation and audit trails.

Change Management

- Develop a change management strategy.

- Identify key stakeholders and champions for AI adoption.

- Communicate the vision and benefits of AI to the entire organization.

- Prepare for employee resistance and have strategies to mitigate it.

Implementation Roadmap

- Decide on a phased approach or full-scale implementation.

- Develop timelines and milestones.

- Allocate responsibilities among teams and leaders.

- Choose the AI technologies and platforms to use.

Pilot Testing

- Select a subset of the operations for initial testing.

- Define metrics to evaluate the pilot's success.

- Monitor the pilot in real-time and make adjustments as needed.

Monitoring and Maintenance

- Set up monitoring tools for performance tracking.

- Establish regular maintenance and update schedules.

- Prepare contingency plans for failures and security breaches.

Future Scalability and Sustainability

- Review the scalability of the solution.

- Plan for ongoing training of machine learning models.

- Create an innovation roadmap for future AI technologies.

By checking off these items, you're not just preparing for AI adoption—you're positioning your business to make the most out of this transformative technology. This exhaustive checklist ensures that every angle is considered, minimizing risks and setting the stage for the effective implementation of AI in your business strategy.

Chapter Seven

Resource Inventory

P reparing for AI Adoption

As you venture into the AI-driven landscape, it's vital to have a comprehensive inventory of all resources at your disposal. This inventory will serve as the foundation upon which your AI initiatives are built, ensuring that you are well-prepared to move ahead. Below is a guide to creating a resource inventory for AI adoption.

Hardware Resources

Computing Power

- Servers: List all servers, including their specifications like CPUs, GPUs, and RAM.

- Workstations: Document all workstations that could be used for lighter AI tasks.

- Specialized Hardware: Inventory any specialized hardware like TPUs or FPGAs.

Networking Equipment

- Routers and switches: List all network hardware and capabilities.

- Firewalls: Document all security hardware and associated rules.

Storage Solutions

- Local Storage: Inventory all local storage solutions like NAS, SAN, or data centers.

- Cloud Storage: Document cloud storage solutions, including providers and available space.

Software Resources

Operating Systems

- List all the operating systems in use and their versions.

Data Management Software

- Databases: List all database software, both SQL and NoSQL.

- Data Warehouses: Inventory any data warehouse solutions.

Development Environments

- IDEs: List all integrated development environments in use.

- Frameworks: Document machine learning frameworks that are already purchased or available for use.

Human Resources

Internal Talent

- Data Scientists: List existing employees with data science skills.

- Developers: Document software developers capable of working on AI projects.

- Business Analysts: Inventory staff who can translate business needs into technical requirements.

External Consultants

- List any external consultants or advisors who can assist in AI adoption.

Financial Resources

- Budget: Document the budget allocated for AI initiatives.

- Grants: List any external grants or funding specifically for AI projects.

Data Resources

Data Types and Sources

- Structured Data: List all sources of structured data like databases.

- Unstructured Data: Document sources of unstructured data like text, images, or videos.

Data Governance Policies

- Access Control: Inventory existing data governance policies regarding who has access to what data.

- Data Usage Policies: Document policies on how data can be used and for what purpose.

Regulatory and Compliance Resources

- Existing Policies: Inventory any existing compliance and regulatory policies that might affect AI adoption.

- Legal Advisors: List internal or external legal advisors familiar with data regulations.

Additional Resources

- Training Material: Inventory any existing training material or platforms that can help staff get up to speed with AI.

- Partnerships: List existing or potential partnerships that could facilitate AI adoption, such as with universities or AI vendors.

Creating a detailed resource inventory will provide you with a panoramic view of what you have, what you need, and how to bridge the gap between the two. This inventory will be an invaluable tool as you plan and execute your AI adoption strategy.

Chapter Eight

Creating an AI-Driven Business Strategy

G oal Setting and SWOT Analysis

Introduction

Artificial Intelligence (AI) is radically altering the landscape of modern business, offering transformative solutions that can redefine how organizations operate, compete, and deliver value. However, implementing AI into your business is not just about adopting a set of new technologies. It's about creating an AI-driven business strategy that aligns with your organization's long-term objectives. This comprehensive guide aims to provide a deep dive into the critical components of such a strategy, with a focus on Goal Setting and SWOT Analysis.

Goal Setting in an AI-Driven Business Strategy

Setting Clear Objectives

The first step in creating an AI-driven business strategy is defining clear objectives. These could be as broad as "improving customer satisfaction" or as specific as "reducing operational costs by 20% within the next two years." The goals serve as the foundation upon which the rest of the AI strategy is built.

SMART Goals

The SMART framework is an effective tool for goal setting. It advocates that goals should be Specific, Measurable, Achievable, Relevant, and Time-bound. Applying the SMART framework to AI-related goals ensures that they are clearly defined and actionable.

Examples:

- Specific: "We aim to automate 70% of customer service interactions using chatbots."

- Measurable: "Reduce customer wait time to under two minutes."

- Achievable: "Deploy a recommendation engine to increase sales by 15%."

- Relevant: "Automate supply chain management to align with increased production targets."

- Time-bound: "Implement predictive maintenance within six months to reduce machine downtime."

Prioritizing Goals

Once you've established your SMART goals, the next step is prioritization. Utilize tools like the Eisenhower Matrix or the MoSCoW method to distinguish between what's urgent and what's important, what must be done, should be done, could be done, and what should be set aside.

SWOT Analysis in an AI-Driven Business Strategy

What is SWOT?

SWOT stands for Strengths, Weaknesses, Opportunities, and Threats. Conducting a SWOT analysis provides you with an organized method to evaluate your business's position relative to AI adoption.

Strengths

Strengths are the existing capabilities that give you a competitive advantage. These could be proprietary technologies, skilled personnel, or data assets. Understanding your strengths allows you to identify where AI can add the most value.

Examples:

- An existing team of data scientists who can accelerate AI adoption.

- A robust IT infrastructure that can support the computational needs of AI algorithms.

Weaknesses

Weaknesses are areas where your business could improve. They are hurdles you will need to overcome to successfully implement AI.

Examples:

- Legacy systems that are incompatible with modern AI technologies.

- A lack of in-house AI expertise.

Opportunities

Opportunities are external factors that you can capitalize on. In the context of AI, these could be emerging technologies, trends, or even regulatory shifts that make AI adoption more feasible or necessary.

Examples:

- The availability of pre-trained AI models that can reduce time-to-market.

- Growing consumer preference for personalized experiences.

Threats

Threats are external factors that could negatively affect your business. These could be competitive moves, changing customer behaviors, or new regulations.

Examples:

- Competitors who have already adopted AI and gained a first-mover advantage.

- Regulatory changes that impose stringent data usage restrictions.

Using SWOT to Inform Strategy

Once the SWOT analysis is complete, the insights should be used to inform your AI strategy. Leverage strengths and opportunities to achieve your goals while formulating plans to address weaknesses and mitigate threats.

Closing Remarks

Creating an AI-driven business strategy is a comprehensive process that goes beyond simply adopting new technologies. It's about aligning your organizational goals with the vast capabilities that AI offers. By setting well-defined, SMART goals and conducting a thorough SWOT analysis, you create a solid foundation for adopting AI in a way that is not just technologically sound but also strategically aligned with your business objectives. The end result is a holistic AI strategy that positions your business for success in the increasingly competitive, AI-driven world.

Chapter Nine

Measuring ROI and Key Performance Indicators

F inancial Metrics and Customer Engagement Metrics

Introduction

As businesses increasingly integrate Artificial Intelligence (AI) into their operational fabric, understanding the Return on Investment (ROI) and the Key Performance Indicators (KPIs) is vital. These metrics help businesses quantify the impact of AI initiatives, informing future strategies and justifying the investment to stakeholders. This guide offers an exhaustive examination of how to measure ROI and

KPIs, focusing specifically on Financial Metrics and Customer Engagement Metrics.

Measuring ROI in AI Initiatives

What is ROI?

Return on Investment, or ROI, is a financial metric used to evaluate the profitability of an investment. For AI projects, ROI is calculated by taking the net gain from the investment and dividing it by the total cost of the project.

$$ROI = (TotalCostofAIProject)(NetProfit) \times 100$$

ROI Factors for AI

- **Costs**: Includes hardware, software, human resources, and ongoing maintenance.

- **Net Gain**: Increased revenue, reduced operational costs, or other quantifiable gains attributable to the AI initiative.

Timeline for ROI Measurement

AI projects often have long incubation periods. Consider short-term, mid-term, and long-term ROI metrics to capture the full impact of your AI initiatives.

Financial Metrics

Operational Cost Savings

- **Automated Processes**: Calculate the cost savings from automating manual tasks.

- **Energy Efficiency**: Measure the reduction in energy consumption from optimized processes.

Increased Revenue

- **Sales Uplift**: Calculate the percentage increase in sales due to personalized recommendations.

- **Customer Lifetime Value**: Analyze how AI has helped increase the average spending of a customer over time.

Cost Avoidance

- **Predictive Maintenance**: Calculate the costs avoided due to minimized downtime.

- **Fraud Detection**: Quantify the amount saved by preventing fraudulent activities.

Customer Engagement Metrics

Customer Retention Rate

Calculate the percentage of customers who continue to engage with your business over a specific period. A higher rate typically indicates successful AI implementations in customer service or personalized marketing.

Net Promoter Score (NPS)

NPS measures customer loyalty and satisfaction. AI can help improve NPS by personalizing customer experiences and offering more efficient services.

Customer Response Time

Measure how AI implementations in customer service, like chatbots, have affected the average response time.

User Engagement on Platforms

- **Click-Through Rates**: Measure the effectiveness of AI-driven personalized advertising or content suggestions.

- **Average Session Duration**: Use this metric to understand how long users are engaging with your AI-enhanced platform.

KPI Dashboards

For real-time tracking and reporting, implement KPI dashboards that focus on the financial metrics and customer engagement metrics.

Tools like Tableau, Microsoft Power BI, and Google Data Studio can be integrated with AI algorithms for real-time analytics.

Future Forecasting

Utilize AI to predict future ROIs and KPIs. Machine learning models can analyze patterns in your metrics and provide forecasts, helping you adjust your strategy proactively.

Conclusion

Measuring ROI and KPIs for AI projects is not just a one-time activity but an ongoing process. Financial metrics allow you to quantify the monetary impact, while customer engagement metrics offer insights into how AI is affecting your customer interactions. Combining these metrics provides a comprehensive view of your AI initiative's effectiveness, helping you make data-driven decisions and optimize your AI-driven business strategy for long-term success.

Chapter Ten

Talent and Team Structure

N avigating Human Capital in an AI-Driven Business

Introduction

In the rapidly evolving landscape of AI-driven business, talent acquisition and team structure become focal points for strategic planning. Effective integration of AI into business operations requires a harmonious blend of skills, roles, and responsibilities, tailored to meet both technical and business goals. This exhaustive guide elaborates on how to build an AI team, role definitions, skill sets, and considerations for in-house versus outsourcing options.

Building an AI Team: Roles and Responsibilities

Data Scientists

Role: Data Scientists are responsible for building and optimizing machine learning models. They engage in data preprocessing, feature engineering, and model evaluation.

Responsibilities:

- Data cleaning and preprocessing

- Model development

- Validation and evaluation of models

Machine Learning Engineers

Role: Machine Learning Engineers take data science models from the lab to a production environment. They ensure the model's scalability and stability.

Responsibilities:

- Code optimization

- Model deployment

- Monitoring model performance in real-time

Data Engineers

Role: Data Engineers create and maintain the architecture that allows for data gathering and storage.

Responsibilities:

- Building data pipelines

- Managing databases and data storage solutions

- Ensuring data quality and integrity

Business Analysts

Role: Business Analysts bridge the gap between AI technology and business needs. They translate business problems into data questions.

Responsibilities:

- Requirement gathering

- KPI identification

- ROI analysis

AI Project Manager

Role: AI Project Managers are responsible for overseeing the project from inception to completion. They handle scheduling, budgeting, and stakeholder communication.

Responsibilities:

- Project scoping

- Team coordination

- Budget and timeline management

Job Descriptions and Skill Sets

Data Scientists

- **Skills**: Python/R, Data Visualization, Statistical Analysis

- **Qualifications**: Master's or Ph.D. in Data Science, Computer Science, or related field

Machine Learning Engineers

- **Skills**: Python, Scala, Deep Learning Frameworks like TensorFlow or PyTorch

- **Qualifications**: Bachelor's in Computer Science, Engineering, or related field

Data Engineers

- **Skills**: SQL, Data Warehousing, Apache Spark

- **Qualifications**: Bachelor's in Computer Science or Engineering

Business Analysts

- **Skills**: Business Intelligence Tools, Basic SQL, Financial Analysis

- **Qualifications**: MBA or Master's in a related business field

AI Project Manager

- **Skills**: Project Management Software, AI Domain Knowledge, Communication Skills

- **Qualifications**: Certification in Project Management, experience in AI projects

In-house vs. Outsourcing

In-house Advantages

- **Control**: Full control over the project scope, quality, and timelines.

- **Intellectual Property**: All created assets remain within the organization.

- **Team Alignment**: Better understanding of company culture and objectives.

In-house Disadvantages

- **Cost**: High upfront costs in talent acquisition and retention.

- **Time**: Takes time to assemble a qualified team and get them up to speed.

Outsourcing Advantages

- **Speed**: Quick deployment since the external team is already specialized.

- **Cost-Efficient**: Reduced overhead and no long-term commitment.

Outsourcing Disadvantages

- **Quality**: Risk of lower quality or misalignment with business objectives.

- **Confidentiality**: Potential risks around data security and intellectual property.

Conclusion

Creating the ideal AI team requires meticulous planning around roles, responsibilities, and the particular skill sets required for those roles. It also necessitates strategic decision-making on sourcing talent, whether it's from within the organization or from external vendors. By having a clear understanding of each role's responsibilities, required skill sets, and the advantages and disadvantages of in-house versus outsourced options, businesses can assemble a team that not only possesses the technical skills but also aligns closely with the organization's business objectives. Such a well-crafted team is crucial for successfully navigating the complexities and opportunities presented by AI in the business environment.

Chapter Eleven

Training and Development for AI Skills

W orkshops and Certification Programs

Introduction

As businesses continue to integrate AI into their operational and strategic frameworks, the onus falls on organizations to equip their teams with the necessary skill sets. While hiring qualified professionals is crucial, it is equally important to focus on the training and development of existing staff to stay ahead of the technological curve. This comprehensive guide delves into the areas of Workshops and Certification Programs as methods for building AI capabilities within an organization.

Workshops

Importance of Workshops

Workshops provide hands-on experiences and practical knowledge. They are beneficial for quickly upskilling employees in specific areas, be it data analytics, machine learning, or AI ethics.

Types of Workshops

1. **Introductory Workshops**: Aimed at beginners, these workshops cover the basics of AI and machine learning, offering a foundation to build upon.

2. **Technical Workshops**: Designed for those who already have a foundational understanding, these delve deeper into coding, algorithms, and technical aspects.

3. **Domain-Specific Workshops**: These are tailored for specific sectors like healthcare, finance, or retail, focusing on the application of AI in those fields.

4. **Ethics and Compliance Workshops**: These workshops discuss the ethical implications of AI and how to adhere to regulatory norms.

Implementing Workshops

- **Duration**: Workshops can range from half-day events to week-long intensive courses.

- **Content**: The curriculum should be well-planned, ideally with input from both business leaders and technical experts.

- **Assessment**: Include tests or projects to evaluate the effectiveness of the workshop.

Certification Programs

Importance of Certification

Certifications offer a structured learning path and result in a qualification that can be added to professional profiles. They offer in-depth knowledge and are usually globally recognized.

Types of Certifications

1. **Basic Certifications**: These cover the fundamentals of AI and machine learning.

2. **Advanced Certifications**: These delve deeper into specialized AI technologies like neural networks, natural language processing, or robotics.

3. **Industry-Specific Certifications**: These are tailored for AI applications in specific industries.

4. **Vendor-Specific Certifications**: Offered by companies like IBM, Microsoft, or Google, these certifications focus on particular tools or platforms.

Implementing Certification Programs

- **Partnerships**: Organizations can partner with educational institutes or specialized AI training centers for certifications.

- **Online vs. Offline**: Consider whether the certification should be offered online, in-person, or in a hybrid format.

- **Duration**: Certification programs usually last several months and require a substantial time commitment.

Evaluating Training Effectiveness

1. **Pre and Post-Assessment**: Use assessments to gauge the learning curve.

2. **Feedback Mechanism**: Regularly collect feedback from the participants for continuous improvement.

3. **KPI Monitoring**: Monitor KPIs like employee productivity or project success rates to quantify the impact of the training.

Conclusion

In the AI-driven landscape, the capabilities of your team can make or break your competitive edge. Workshops and Certification Programs offer different yet complementary ways to build AI skills within your organization. While workshops are excellent for rapid and focused learning, certification programs offer more in-depth knowledge and a more structured learning path. By implementing a mix of both, organizations can ensure a well-rounded, highly skilled team capable of navigating the complexities and opportunities presented by AI.

Chapter Twelve

Data
Infrastructure
and Engineering

D ata Acquisition Strategies, Web Scraping, and APIs

Introduction

In the context of AI-driven businesses, data serves as the lifeblood that fuels machine learning models and data analytics processes. The task of setting up a robust data infrastructure, therefore, becomes critical. This comprehensive guide focuses on Data Infrastructure and Engineering with a particular emphasis on Data Acquisition Strategies, Web Scraping, and APIs.

Data Infrastructure and Engineering

Importance

Data infrastructure encompasses the technologies and architecture that facilitate the collection, storage, and processing of data. Without a robust infrastructure, your AI models are as good as non-functional.

Key Components

1. **Data Lakes & Data Warehouses**: Central repositories for storing raw and structured data respectively.

2. **Data Pipelines**: Automate the flow of data from multiple sources to storage or analytical tools.

3. **Computational Resources**: Hardware and cloud resources to run data processing and machine learning algorithms.

Data Acquisition Strategies

First-Party Data

- **Definition**: Data generated from your own business operations, such as user interaction data or sales data.

- **Methods**: Log files, database records, CRM systems.

Third-Party Data

- **Definition**: Data purchased or acquired from external sources.

- **Methods**: Data vendors, partnerships, open-source data sets.

Real-Time Data

- **Definition**: Data that is collected and processed in real-time.

- **Methods**: Sensors, IoT devices, real-time analytics platforms.

Web Scraping

What is Web Scraping?

Web scraping is the method of extracting data from websites. It's a valuable technique for gathering data that is publicly available but not easily downloadable.

Tools and Libraries

- **Beautiful Soup**: A Python library for web scraping purposes to pull the data out of HTML and XML files.

- **Selenium**: Primarily used for automating web applications for testing purposes but is also useful for general web scraping.

Legal and Ethical Concerns

- **Robot.txt**: Always check a website's robot.txt file for guidance on what is allowed to be scraped.

- **Data Privacy Laws**: Be aware of data privacy regulations such as GDPR or CCPA.

APIs (Application Programming Interfaces)

What are APIs?

APIs are sets of protocols and tools for building software applications. They define methods for requesting data from servers, making them an excellent resource for data acquisition.

Types of APIs

1. **RESTful APIs**: The most common type of web API, offering CRUD (Create, Read, Update, Delete) functionalities.

2. **Streaming APIs**: These are used for real-time data acquisition, commonly seen in social media platforms like Twitter.

Rate Limiting and Quotas

APIs often have usage restrictions, and it's crucial to be aware of rate limits and quotas to avoid being temporarily or permanently banned from using the service.

Conclusion

In the digital age where data is an invaluable asset, the importance of having a robust data infrastructure cannot be overstated. From data acquisition strategies involving first-party, third-party, and real-time data, to data harvesting techniques like web scraping and APIs, a multi-faceted approach is essential. These methods, when executed correctly, provide the raw material that fuels your AI algorithms, driving your business towards informed decision-making and operational excellence.

Chapter Thirteen

Data Storage and Database Management

S QL vs. NoSQL, Cloud Storage Solutions

Introduction

In the digital world, the ability to store, manage, and query data is a cornerstone of any AI-driven business strategy. The choices you make in terms of data storage and database management can directly influence how efficiently you can harness data for your business. This exhaustive guide delves into SQL vs. NoSQL databases and explores the different cloud storage solutions available in the market.

SQL vs. NoSQL Databases

SQL Databases

What are SQL Databases?

SQL (Structured Query Language) databases are relational databases that use structured query language for defining and manipulating the data.

Advantages

1. **ACID Compliance**: Ensures reliability in every transaction.

2. **Complex Queries**: Ability to perform complex queries and joins.

3. **Schema**: SQL databases require a predefined schema.

Use-cases

- Financial systems

- Customer Relationship Management (CRM)

- Enterprise Resource Planning (ERP)

Popular SQL Databases

- MySQL

- PostgreSQL

- Microsoft SQL Server

NoSQL Databases

What are NoSQL Databases?

NoSQL databases are non-relational and can store structured, semi-structured, or unstructured data. They do not require a fixed schema.

Advantages

1. **Scalability**: Easily scalable both horizontally and vertically.

2. **Flexibility**: No need for a fixed schema and the data can be inserted without first defining its structure.

3. **High Throughput**: Efficiently handles large data volumes and real-time analytics.

Use-cases

- Real-time analytics

- Internet of Things (IoT)

- Content Management Systems

Popular NoSQL Databases

- MongoDB

- Cassandra

- Couchbase

Cloud Storage Solutions

Importance of Cloud Storage

Storing data in the cloud can provide scalable, secure, and cost-efficient data storage solutions. It allows businesses to focus on data utilization rather than the intricacies of data management.

Types of Cloud Storage

1. **Object Storage**: Ideal for unstructured data like multimedia files. Example: Amazon S3.

2. **File Storage**: Used for hierarchical data storage needs. Example: Azure File Storage.

3. **Block Storage**: Best suited for databases or other block-based storage needs. Example: Amazon EBS.

Factors to Consider

1. **Security**: Encryption, Access Controls, Compliance with data protection regulations.

2. **Cost**: Storage costs, retrieval costs, data transfer costs.

3. **Scalability**: Ability to scale storage capacity according to business needs.

Popular Cloud Storage Providers

- Amazon Web Services (AWS)

- Google Cloud Platform (GCP)

- Microsoft Azure

Conclusion

Choosing the right data storage and database management solutions is a pivotal decision for any AI-driven business. While SQL databases are excellent for transactional data and complex queries, NoSQL databases offer more flexibility and scalability, especially for unstructured or semi-structured data. On the other hand, cloud storage solutions offer secure and scalable options for data storage, making it easier for businesses to focus on leveraging data for actionable insights. Therefore, understanding the nuances of each of these options can help businesses craft a robust data infrastructure that aligns with their specific needs.

Chapter Fourteen

Data Cleaning, Transformation, and Preprocessing

M issing Data and Data Normalization

Introduction

Before data can be used to generate insights or fuel machine learning algorithms, it often needs to be cleaned, transformed, and preprocessed. Raw data usually contains a host of problems, ranging from missing values to inconsistencies. This comprehensive guide dives into the critical aspects of data cleaning, transformation, and preprocessing, with a special focus on handling missing data and data normalization.

Data Cleaning

What is Data Cleaning?

Data cleaning involves the correction or removal of inaccuracies in datasets. This is crucial for ensuring that the eventual analysis is accurate and meaningful.

Importance of Data Cleaning

- **Improves Accuracy**: Dirty data can mislead and result in false insights.

- **Enhances Productivity**: Clean data minimizes time spent on dealing with data quality issues during analysis.

Techniques

- **Outlier Detection and Removal**: Identifying and removing extreme values that deviate from other observations.

- **Duplicate Removal**: Identifying and eliminating redundant records.

Missing Data

What is Missing Data?

Data can have missing values for a variety of reasons, ranging from human errors during data collection to inconsistencies in source systems.

Techniques to Handle Missing Data

1. **Listwise Deletion**: Removing any row with at least one missing value.

2. **Imputation**: Filling in the missing values based on other observations.

   o **Mean/Median/Mode Imputation**: Replace missing values with the mean, median, or mode of the column.

   o **K-Nearest Neighbors**: Using the k-nearest observations to impute the missing values.

Potential Pitfalls

- **Bias**: Incorrect handling can introduce bias into the dataset.

- **Loss of Information**: Deleting rows may result in a loss of useful information.

Data Transformation and Preprocessing

What is Data Transformation?

Data transformation involves converting data into a suitable format or structure for analysis.

Techniques

- **Encoding Categorical Variables**: Converting categories into a format that can be provided to machine learning algorithms.

- **Feature Scaling**: Modifying the scale of variables so they can be compared on common grounds.

Data Normalization

What is Data Normalization?

Data normalization is the process of rescaling features to a standard range.

Techniques

1. **Min-Max Scaling**: Rescales features to lie in a given range, usually [0,1].

2. **Z-score Normalization**: Transforms features to have a mean of 0 and a standard deviation of 1.

When to Use Normalization?

- **Distance-Based Algorithms**: Such as K-NN and SVM.

- **Gradient Descent-Based Algorithms**: Such as neural networks.

Conclusion

Data cleaning, transformation, and preprocessing are foundational steps in the data pipeline. Dealing effectively with missing data ensures that you are not making decisions based on incomplete or biased information. Likewise, data normalization is often an essential step for algorithms that are sensitive to the scale of the input features. By giving due attention to these aspects, you lay the groundwork for more advanced analyses and predictive models, thereby better leveraging your data for decision-making and strategy formulation.

Chapter Fifteen

Algorithms, Models, and Applications

D eep Dive into AI Algorithms: Supervised Learning and Unsupervised Learning

Introduction

Artificial Intelligence (AI) has revolutionized the business landscape, offering a range of solutions for automating tasks, generating insights, and making data-driven decisions. At the heart of these AI systems are algorithms that enable machines to learn from data. This comprehensive guide will delve deep into two primary categories of machine learning algorithms: Supervised Learning and Unsupervised Learning.

Supervised Learning

What is Supervised Learning?

Supervised Learning is a type of machine learning paradigm where the model is trained on labeled data. The data is provided with the answer key, and the algorithm iteratively makes predictions and is corrected when its predictions are incorrect.

Common Algorithms

1. **Linear Regression**: Used for predicting a continuous output variable.

2. **Logistic Regression**: Used for classification tasks.

3. **Decision Trees**: Used for both classification and regression tasks.

4. **Random Forests**: An ensemble of decision trees.

5. **Support Vector Machines**: Effective in high-dimensional spaces.

Applications

- Predicting Customer Churn

- Email Spam Filtering

- Real Estate Price Prediction

Challenges and Pitfalls

- **Overfitting**: When the model learns the noise in the data.

- **Data Imbalance**: The model may perform poorly on under-represented classes.

Evaluation Metrics

- **Accuracy**: The ratio of correctly predicted observation to the total observations.

- **Precision and Recall**: Precision is the ratio of correctly predicted positive observations to the total predicted positives. Recall is the ratio of correctly predicted positive observations to all the actual positives.

Unsupervised Learning

What is Unsupervised Learning?

Unsupervised Learning involves training the machine using data that is neither classified nor labeled, allowing the algorithm to act on the data without guidance.

Common Algorithms

1. **K-Means Clustering**: Divides the data into 'K' number of clusters.

2. **Hierarchical Clustering**: Builds a tree of clusters.

3. **Principal Component Analysis (PCA)**: Reduces the dimensionality of the data.

4. **Anomaly Detection**: Identifies outliers or anomalies in the data.

Applications

- Customer Segmentation

- Recommendation Systems

- Fraud Detection

Challenges and Pitfalls

- **Choosing K in K-means**: Determining the number of clusters.

- **Noisy Data**: Noise can have a more significant impact than in supervised learning.

Evaluation Metrics

- **Silhouette Score**: Measures how similar an object is to its own cluster compared to other clusters.

- **Davies-Bouldin Index**: The average similarity ratio of each cluster with the cluster most similar to it.

Conclusion

Supervised and Unsupervised Learning offer unique advantages and challenges that make them suitable for different kinds of tasks. While supervised learning is excellent for targeted outcomes, unsupervised learning excels at uncovering hidden patterns in the data. Understanding the intricacies of these algorithms will not only facilitate better model selection but also significantly improve your AI-driven initiatives.

Specialized Business Algorithms: Time-Series Forecasting and Anomaly Detection

Introduction

In today's competitive business landscape, companies are increasingly looking to specialized algorithms to gain an edge. Algorithms tailored to specific business applications can yield insights that generic algorithms overlook. This comprehensive guide dives into two such specialized business algorithms: Time-Series Forecasting and Anomaly Detection.

Time-Series Forecasting

What is Time-Series Forecasting?

Time-Series Forecasting involves using historical data points to predict future values of a series over time. This is especially useful in finance, sales, and inventory management.

Common Algorithms

1. **ARIMA (AutoRegressive Integrated Moving Average)**: Combines autoregression, differencing, and moving average components.

2. **Prophet**: Developed by Facebook, suitable for daily observations with missing data and outliers.

3. **LSTM (Long Short-Term Memory)**: A type of recurrent neural network suitable for sequence prediction.

Applications in Business

- Stock Price Prediction

- Sales Forecasting

- Inventory Level Prediction

Challenges and Pitfalls

- **Seasonality**: Failing to account for seasonal patterns can result in inaccurate forecasts.

- **Overfitting**: Overcomplicating the model can make it poorly generalize to future data.

Evaluation Metrics

- **RMSE (Root Mean Square Error)**: Measures the average magnitude of forecast errors.

- **MAPE (Mean Absolute Percentage Error)**: Expresses forecast error as a percentage.

Anomaly Detection

What is Anomaly Detection?

Anomaly Detection is the identification of rare items, events, or observations that raise suspicions by differing significantly from the majority of the data.

Common Algorithms

1. **Isolation Forest**: An ensemble learning algorithm for anomaly detection.

2. **One-Class SVM**: Useful for high-dimensional data.

3. **K-Nearest Neighbors (K-NN)**: Classifies a data point

based on its nearest neighbors.

Applications in Business

- Fraud Detection

- Quality Assurance in Manufacturing

- Network Security

Challenges and Pitfalls

- **Imbalanced Data**: Anomalies are rare events, making the data highly imbalanced.

- **Feature Engineering**: Incorrect features can lead to false positives or false negatives.

Evaluation Metrics

- **Precision-Recall Curve**: Useful when classes are imbalanced.

- **F1-Score**: The harmonic mean of precision and recall.

Conclusion

Time-Series Forecasting and Anomaly Detection are specialized algorithms that can offer invaluable insights for specific business applications. Time-series forecasting is indispensable for planning and strategy, particularly when historical data is a good indicator of future events. Anomaly detection is crucial for identifying events that don't conform to expected patterns, such as fraud or system intrusions. Understanding the nuances and applications of these specialized algorithms can empower your business to make more informed decisions, improve planning, and enhance security measures.

Natural Language Processing for Customer Service: Chatbots and Sentiment Analysis

Introduction

The rise of Natural Language Processing (NLP) technologies has revolutionized customer service. Automating customer interactions and understanding customer sentiments have never been easier. In this comprehensive guide, we'll delve deep into two major applications of NLP in customer service: Chatbots and Sentiment Analysis.

Chatbots

What are Chatbots?

Chatbots are AI-driven software applications that can simulate a conversation with human users. They interpret and process the user's words and provide instant pre-set answers.

Common Algorithms

1. **Rule-Based Approaches**: Simple chatbots based on predefined rules and pathways.

2. **Machine Learning-Based**: These bots use algorithms like Naive Bayes or Support Vector Machines to improve their responses.

3. **Deep Learning-Based**: Utilizing Recurrent Neural Networks (RNNs) or Transformers for more advanced conversations.

Applications in Customer Service

- Automated Customer Support

- Lead Generation

- Personalized Recommendations

Challenges and Pitfalls

- **Context Management**: Maintaining a conversation's context over an extended interaction.

- **Handling Ambiguity**: Determining the correct response when queries are unclear.

Evaluation Metrics

- **Customer Satisfaction Score (CSAT)**: A metric that

gauges customer satisfaction from interactions.

- **Response Time**: The time taken to provide a reply.

Sentiment Analysis

What is Sentiment Analysis?

Sentiment Analysis refers to the use of NLP to identify and categorize opinions expressed in a piece of text, especially to determine whether the writer's attitude is positive, negative, or neutral.

Common Algorithms

1. **Naive Bayes**: A probabilistic algorithm often used for text classification.

2. **Random Forest**: A robust algorithm that can handle a variety of data types.

3. **LSTM**: Long Short-Term Memory networks, useful for sequence prediction like time-series sentiment analysis over a text.

Applications in Customer Service

- Monitoring Customer Feedback

- Product Reviews

- Crisis Management

Challenges and Pitfalls

- **Sarcasm and Irony**: These can easily be misinterpreted by algorithms.

- **Language and Cultural Nuances**: Language-specific idioms and cultural context can alter sentiment interpretation.

Evaluation Metrics

- **Precision, Recall, and F1-Score**: These metrics are vital for measuring the effectiveness of a classification model.

- **Accuracy**: Though commonly used, it can be misleading if the data is imbalanced.

Conclusion

NLP technologies like Chatbots and Sentiment Analysis have significant implications for enhancing customer service. Chatbots can provide fast, around-the-clock support, while Sentiment Analysis can offer deep insights into customer attitudes and perceptions. Understanding the intricacies and limitations of these technologies is crucial for maximizing their utility and optimizing customer experiences.

Recommender Systems for Product and Service Optimization: Content-Based and Collaborative Filtering

Introduction

In a digital age where consumers are overwhelmed with choices, recommender systems have emerged as a game-changing tool for product and service optimization. They not only assist users in making choices but also help businesses to personalize offers, thereby increasing sales and customer satisfaction. This guide takes a deep dive into two core types of recommender systems: Content-Based and Collaborative Filtering.

Content-Based Recommender Systems

What are Content-Based Recommender Systems?

Content-Based Recommender Systems focus on the attributes of items and a profile of the user's preferences. These systems recommend items similar to what the user likes, based on their past actions or explicit feedback.

Common Algorithms

1. **TF-IDF (Term Frequency-Inverse Document Frequency)**: Weighs the importance of different words in a dataset.

2. **Cosine Similarity**: Measures how similar two vectors are.

3. **Decision Trees**: Used for rule-based categorization of items.

Applications in Business

- Product Recommendations

- Personalized Email Marketing

- Tailored News Feeds

Challenges and Pitfalls

- **Limited Scope**: Only recommends items similar to what the user has previously interacted with.

- **Over-Specialization**: May lead to a filter bubble where users are not exposed to differing content.

Evaluation Metrics

- **Precision@k**: Measures how many of the top-k recommended items are relevant.

- **Recall@k**: Measures how many of the relevant items appear in the top-k recommendations.

Collaborative Filtering

What is Collaborative Filtering?

Collaborative Filtering systems recommend items based on the likes and dislikes of users in the past and find similarities between the users for making recommendations.

Common Algorithms

1. **User-User Collaborative Filtering**: Finds similar users and recommend items that those similar users have liked.

2. **Item-Item Collaborative Filtering**: Identifies similar items based on users' past interactions.

3. **Matrix Factorization Methods**: SVD, ALS, and others that decompose the user-item interaction matrix.

Applications in Business

- Movie Recommendations

- Cross-Selling in E-Commerce

- Personalized Online Advertising

Challenges and Pitfalls

- **Cold Start Problem**: New users or items with little to no interaction data are challenging to recommend.

- **Scalability**: Computing similarities can become resource-intensive as the dataset grows.

Evaluation Metrics

- **RMSE (Root Mean Square Error)**: Measures the average of the squares of the errors between predicted and actual ratings.

- **MAE (Mean Absolute Error)**: Measures the average absolute errors between the predicted and actual ratings.

Conclusion

Both Content-Based and Collaborative Filtering have unique strengths and weaknesses, making them suited for different kinds of recommendation challenges. While Content-Based systems are excellent for providing targeted recommendations based on item characteristics, Collaborative Filtering excels in leveraging user interactions for broader, yet personalized recommendations. Understanding both approaches allows businesses to create more effective, hybrid recommender systems that enhance user engagement and optimize product and service offerings.

Chapter Sixteen

Sector-Specific Case Studies

A pplications of AI in Various Industries: A Comprehensive Guide

Introduction

Artificial Intelligence (AI) has become a transformative force that is reshaping various industries. Its applications range from enhancing customer experiences to optimizing operational efficiencies. This guide provides an exhaustive overview of how AI impacts key sectors like Retail, Healthcare, Finance, Manufacturing, and Supply Chain Management.

Retail: From Inventory Management to Personalization

Inventory Management

- **Algorithmic Forecasting**: AI algorithms help forecast demand and inventory levels with high accuracy.

- **Automated Reordering**: AI systems can automate the reordering process based on real-time inventory levels.

Personalization

- **Customer Segmentation**: Machine learning algorithms segment customers based on purchasing behaviors.

- **Recommendation Engines**: Leveraging collaborative filtering and content-based algorithms to offer personalized suggestions.

Healthcare: Diagnostics to Remote Monitoring

Diagnostics

- **Image Recognition**: AI algorithms like CNNs are used for detecting anomalies in X-rays and MRIs.

- **Predictive Analytics**: Machine learning models predict patient risks based on historical data.

Remote Monitoring

- **Wearable Devices**: AI-powered wearables monitor various health metrics in real-time.

- **Telemedicine**: AI assists in remote patient consultation and follow-ups.

Finance: Risk Management, Fraud Detection, and Algorithmic Trading

Risk Management

- **Credit Scoring**: Machine learning algorithms analyze customer data to assess credit risk.

- **Portfolio Management**: AI-driven optimization for diversified portfolio management.

Fraud Detection and Algorithmic Trading

- **Anomaly Detection**: AI identifies irregular patterns that suggest fraudulent activities.

- **High-Frequency Trading**: Algorithms make rapid trades based on real-time market data.

Manufacturing: Process Optimization and Predictive Maintenance

Process Optimization

- **Quality Assurance**: Machine vision algorithms ensure product quality in real-time.

- **Resource Allocation**: AI algorithms optimize the use of resources in manufacturing processes.

Predictive Maintenance

- **Sensor Data**: AI analyzes sensor data to predict machine failures.

- **Maintenance Scheduling**: Optimization algorithms schedule maintenance activities to minimize downtime.

Supply Chain: Logistics and Route Optimization

Logistics

- **Demand Forecasting**: AI algorithms predict the demand for various products in different regions.

- **Inventory Optimization**: AI helps in maintaining optimal inventory levels.

Route Optimization

- **GPS Data Analysis**: Machine learning models analyze GPS data for optimal route planning.

- **Dynamic Adjustments**: AI systems make real-time adjustments to routes based on various factors like traffic and weather conditions.

Conclusion

AI's role is pivotal in driving innovation and efficiencies across industries. Whether it's enhancing the retail experience through personalization, enabling accurate diagnostics in healthcare, mitigating risks in finance, optimizing processes in manufacturing, or streamlining logistics in supply chain management, AI has proven its versatility and indispensability. Understanding these applications is the first step in harnessing AI's potential to create competitive advantages and operational efficiencies.

Chapter Seventeen

Operationalization and Scaling

P roject Management Frameworks for AI - Agile and Waterfall

Introduction

Operationalizing and scaling AI projects within an organization are critical steps that come after model development. The effectiveness of these steps largely depends on the project management approach adopted. This guide offers an in-depth look at two prevalent project management frameworks for AI—Agile and Waterfall.

Operationalization and Scaling

Key Considerations

- **Model Deployment**: Streamlining the process of putting

trained models into production.

- **Monitoring and Maintenance**: Ensuring that the models are updated and performing optimally.

- **Resource Allocation**: Determining the required resources for large-scale implementation.

- **Team Collaboration**: Facilitating seamless interactions among data scientists, engineers, and business stakeholders.

Best Practices

- **Automation**: Use of MLOps tools for automated model retraining and monitoring.

- **Documentation**: Comprehensive documentation to ensure that the model can be understood and modified in the future.

- **Compliance and Governance**: Adhering to regulatory standards and ethical guidelines.

Project Management Frameworks for AI

Agile Methodology

What is Agile?

Agile is a flexible and iterative approach to software development and project management. It promotes collaborative problem solving, and customer-centricity.

Agile in AI

- **Sprints**: Short development cycles that allow for rapid prototyping and adjustments.

- **User Stories**: Focus on solving specific challenges or delivering specific functionalities during each sprint.

- **Continuous Feedback**: Regular stakeholder and customer feedback to refine the model or features.

Pros and Cons

- **Pros**: Flexibility, quicker time to market, and adaptability.

- **Cons**: Scope creep, less predictability, and potential for increased costs.

Waterfall Methodology

What is Waterfall?

Waterfall is a sequential and rigid framework where each phase must be completed before the next begins.

Waterfall in AI

- **Requirements Gathering**: Comprehensive list of require-ments is established before any development begins.

- **Development and Testing**: Phases strictly follow each oth-er, with each phase depending on the deliverables of the preceding phase.

- **Deployment**: Takes place after all prior phases are satisfac-torily completed.

Pros and Cons

- **Pros**: Clear structure, easier to manage, and defined time-lines.

- **Cons**: Inflexible, long time to market, and changes are costly once the project has started.

Conclusion

The choice between Agile and Waterfall frameworks for managing AI projects depends on various factors including the scale of the pro-ject, the clarity of requirements, and the need for flexibility. Agile is generally better suited for projects where requirements may evolve, whereas Waterfall is ideal for projects with well-defined requirements and compliance constraints. Understanding these frameworks is cru-cial for the successful operationalization and scaling of AI initiatives.

Overcoming Implementation Challenges: Data Inconsistencies and Model Bias

Introduction

Implementation challenges are often the bottlenecks that prevent AI projects from transitioning smoothly from a pilot stage to full-scale deployment. Two of the most common challenges faced are Data Inconsistencies and Model Bias. This guide offers exhaustive insights into identifying and mitigating these challenges effectively.

Data Inconsistencies

What are Data Inconsistencies?

Data inconsistencies arise when data across different systems, formats, or entries do not align. This can severely affect the quality of insights derived from AI models.

Identifying Data Inconsistencies

- **Schema Mismatch**: Inconsistencies in the structure of data across different databases or tables.

- **Duplicate Entries**: Multiple instances of the same data point.

- **Outliers**: Data points that deviate significantly from the rest of the dataset.

Overcoming Data Inconsistencies

1. **Data Auditing**: Periodically review data for inconsistencies.

2. **Data Cleaning Tools**: Use automated tools to clean and preprocess data.

3. **Version Control**: Maintain versions of datasets to track changes over time.

4. **Validation Rules**: Implement rules to validate the data at the point of entry.

Model Bias

What is Model Bias?

Model bias occurs when an algorithmic model makes assumptions that skew its predictions or classifications, leading to unfair or in-equitable outcomes.

Types of Model Bias

- **Data Bias**: Biases present in the training data reflecting historical prejudices.

- **Algorithmic Bias**: Biases introduced by the algorithms or the parameters chosen for model training.

Overcoming Model Bias

1. **Diverse Training Data**: Ensuring the training data represents various groups equitably.

2. **Algorithmic Fairness Techniques**: Use methods like re-sampling, re-weighting, or bias-correction algorithms.

3. **Transparency**: Make the model and its decision-making process as transparent as possible.

4. **External Audits**: Regular external reviews to identify and eliminate any form of bias.

Conclusion

Data Inconsistencies and Model Bias are critical challenges that can undermine the effectiveness of AI implementations. However, they are not insurmountable. Through systematic auditing, cleaning, validation, and fairness techniques, these challenges can be effectively mitigated. By proactively addressing these issues, businesses can significantly improve the robustness, reliability, and fairness of their AI systems, thereby ensuring more successful implementations.

Monitoring, Auditing, and Updating Models: A Comprehensive Guide

Introduction

Once an AI model is deployed into production, the work is far from over. Continuous monitoring, auditing, and updating are essential to ensure that the model remains effective and relevant. This guide delves into these aspects, detailing best practices and strategies for each.

Continuous Monitoring

Importance

- **Model Drift**: Data distributions and relationships change over time, impacting model performance.

- **Error Analysis**: Identifying patterns where the model's predictions are consistently inaccurate.

Best Practices

1. **Real-time Dashboards**: Implement dashboards that track key performance indicators (KPIs) in real-time.

2. **Automated Alerts**: Set up automatic alert systems for anomalies or sudden changes in model performance.

3. **Feedback Loops**: Establish a mechanism to get constant feedback from users and stakeholders.

4. **Health Checks**: Regularly test the model to ensure it's operating as expected.

Tools

- **Monitoring Tools**: Software like Prometheus, Grafana, or custom solutions for real-time tracking.

- **Logging Services**: Use centralized logging services to keep track of model predictions and input features.

Version Control

Importance

- **Reproducibility**: Ensuring that you can return to any previous model version is vital for debugging and auditing.

- **Collaboration**: Makes it easier for team members to collaborate and keep track of changes.

Best Practices

1. **Version Naming**: Use consistent and informative naming conventions for model versions.

2. **Change Logs**: Maintain detailed logs for each change, including the rationale and impact.

3. **Dependency Tracking**: Keep track of the data and dependencies used for each model version.

4. **Archiving**: Periodically archive older versions that are no longer in use but might be needed for auditing or regulatory compliance.

Tools

- **Data Versioning Tools**: Software like DVC or Pachyderm for versioning datasets.

- **Model Versioning Services**: Platforms like MLflow or TensorFlow Model Server for model version management.

Auditing and Updating Models

Auditing

- **Performance Auditing**: Regular checks to compare model predictions against actual outcomes.

- **Fairness Auditing**: Ensure that the model is not biased against certain groups or individuals.

Updating Models

1. **Retraining**: Use updated data to retrain models and improve their accuracy.

2. **Fine-Tuning**: Make minor adjustments to the model parameters rather than training it from scratch.

3. **A/B Testing**: Test the updated model against the current version to measure improvements.

Conclusion

Continuous monitoring, effective version control, and periodic auditing and updates are the backbone of a reliable and robust AI system. By implementing these strategies, organizations can ensure that their models remain accurate, fair, and in line with evolving business objectives.

Chapter Eighteen

Future Trends and Long-Term Strategy

N avigating the AI Landscape

Introduction

As organizations integrate Artificial Intelligence (AI) into their operational fabric, it is crucial to remain forward-looking. Understanding future trends is essential for long-term planning and sustainability. This guide aims to offer an exhaustive overview of what lies ahead, from emerging technologies to regulatory shifts and sustainable practices.

Emerging Technologies: Blockchain, IoT, and Beyond

Blockchain and AI

Blockchain, known for its secure, immutable records, can complement AI by ensuring data integrity and enabling decentralized machine learning models.

- **Smart Contracts**: Automated, self-executing contracts can streamline AI-powered decision-making processes.

- **Data Security**: Blockchain can secure the data supply chain, increasing the trustworthiness of AI models.

Internet of Things (IoT) and AI

IoT devices collect vast amounts of real-time data, which can be leveraged for AI models.

- **Edge Computing**: AI algorithms can run directly on IoT devices, making real-time decisions without the need for cloud connectivity.

- **Predictive Maintenance**: IoT sensors can feed data to AI models that predict equipment failures and schedule timely maintenance.

Beyond Blockchain and IoT

- **Quantum Computing**: Could drastically reduce machine learning computation times.

- **Augmented Reality**: AI could make AR more interactive

and responsive to human behavior.

Sustainability and Eco-Friendly AI

Energy Efficiency

- **Green Algorithms**: Research is ongoing to create algorithms that require less computational power, thereby reducing the carbon footprint.

Eco-Friendly Data Centers

- **Renewable Energy**: Companies are investing in data centers powered by renewable energy to offset the environmental impact.

Ethical and Sustainable AI

- **Resource Optimization**: AI can be used to optimize resource utilization in various industries, reducing waste and environmental impact.

Preparing for Regulatory Changes

Data Privacy

- **GDPR and CCPA**: Understanding and compliance with global data protection laws are crucial for any AI strategy.

Antitrust Laws

- **Monopolistic Practices**: As AI can give companies a considerable edge, antitrust laws may evolve to prevent AI-induced monopolies.

AI Ethics

- **Algorithmic Accountability**: Governments may implement rules holding companies accountable for their algorithms' decisions and biases.

AI in a Post-Pandemic World

Remote Work Optimization

- **Virtual Collaboration**: AI can enhance virtual collaboration tools, making remote work more efficient.

Health and Safety

- **AI-Driven Diagnostics**: Expect a rise in AI applications in healthcare diagnostics.

Supply Chain Resilience

- **Predictive Analytics**: AI can fortify supply chains by predicting disruptions and suggesting mitigations.

Conclusion

The future of AI is incredibly promising but comes with its set of challenges and responsibilities. From new technologies like Blockchain and IoT to impending regulatory changes and sustainability concerns, there is much to consider for long-term strategy. Most importantly, as we navigate through a post-pandemic world, AI has the potential to play a pivotal role in shaping a resilient, inclusive, and sustainable future. Companies that align their AI strategies with these emerging trends will not only stay ahead of the curve but also contribute positively to society at large.

Chapter Nineteen

Resources

Navigating the complex landscape of AI in business requires a rich arsenal of resources. This section compiles an exhaustive list of supplementary materials, toolkits, and educational platforms to accelerate your journey.

Glossary of Technical and Business Terms

1. **Algorithm**: A set of rules to solve a particular problem.

2. **Data Science**: The study of data: its origin, what it represents, and the ways to transform it into valuable insights.

3. **Machine Learning**: A type of AI that enables systems to learn from data.

4. **Blockchain**: A distributed ledger technology for secure and transparent transactions.

5. **IoT (Internet of Things)**: Network of physical objects embedded with sensors, software, and other technologies to

collect and share data.

6. **KPI (Key Performance Indicator)**: A metric used to evaluate factors crucial to an organization's success.

7. **GDPR (General Data Protection Regulation)**: EU legislation that protects the privacy and personal data of individuals.

8. **ROI (Return on Investment)**: A measure of the profitability of an investment.

Recommended Reading, Courses, and Conferences

Reading

1. "Artificial Intelligence: A Guide to Intelligent Systems" by Michael Negnevitsky

2. "Data Science for Business" by Foster Provost and Tom Fawcett

Courses

1. "Machine Learning by Andrew Ng" on Coursera

2. "Professional Certificate in Machine Learning and Artificial Intelligence" from MIT on edX

Conferences

1. NeurIPS (Conference on Neural Information Processing Systems)

2. AI Expo

Toolkits for AI Implementation: Languages and Frameworks

Languages

1. **Python**: Highly recommended for data manipulation and machine learning.

2. **R**: Excellent for statistical analysis and data visualization.

3. **Java**: Used in large-scale systems and Android applications incorporating AI.

Frameworks

1. **TensorFlow**: Open-source library developed by Google, suitable for a variety of AI tasks.

2. **PyTorch**: Known for its dynamic computation graphs, making it particularly useful for deep learning research.

3. **Scikit-learn**: Simple and effective tools for data mining and

data analysis.

Libraries for Specialized Tasks

1. **NLTK**: For natural language processing.

2. **OpenCV**: For computer vision tasks.

3. **Pandas**: For data manipulation and analysis.

By leveraging these resources, you can deepen your understanding, enhance your skills, and stay updated on the latest trends and technologies in the rapidly evolving field of AI in business.

Chapter Twenty

Appendix

The appendix serves as a valuable resource for readers who want a more detailed dive into some of the specific areas discussed throughout the book. It provides practical tools, additional information, and resources that can aid in the planning and implementation stages of an AI project.

Global Data Privacy Regulations

Understanding data privacy regulations is crucial when incorporating AI into business practices. This section provides an overview of important global regulations that impact AI and data management.

1. **GDPR (General Data Protection Regulation)**: European Union's framework for data protection laws.

2. **CCPA (California Consumer Privacy Act)**: Protects the privacy and data of consumers residing in California.

3. **HIPAA (Health Insurance Portability and Accountability Act)**: U.S. legislation that protects sensitive patient

health information.

4. **PIPEDA (Personal Information Protection and Electronic Documents Act)**: Canadian data privacy law.

Chapter Twenty-One

Sample Data Science Project Timelines and Budgets

Incorporating AI into your business requires not just a technical understanding but also a practical approach to timelines and budgets.

1. **Pilot Project**

   - Timeline: 3-6 months

   - Budget: $20,000 - $50,000

2. **Medium-Scale Implementation**

- ○ Timeline: 6-12 months

- ○ Budget: $100,000 - $300,000

3. Enterprise-Level Deployment

- ○ Timeline: 1-2 years

- ○ Budget: $500,000+

Checklists for Evaluating AI Vendors and Solutions

When considering third-party AI solutions, it's essential to evaluate the vendors thoroughly.

Vendor Checklist

1. **Company Profile**: History, mission, and key personnel.

2. **Customer Testimonials**: Look for case studies or client testimonials.

3. **Data Security**: Ask about their data security protocols.

4. **Compliance**: Make sure they comply with global data privacy laws.

5. **Cost**: Breakdown of initial setup fees, monthly or yearly subscriptions, and additional costs.

Solution Checklist

1. **Scalability**: Can the solution grow with your business?

2. **Customization**: How easy is it to tailor the solution to your specific needs?

3. **Integration**: Does it integrate well with your existing systems?

4. **Support**: Types of customer support offered (e.g., 24/7, chat, phone).

5. **Updates and Upgrades**: How frequently is the solution updated?

www.ingramcontent.com/pod-product-compliance
Lightning Source LLC
LaVergne TN
LVHW051700050326
832903LV00032B/3920